Every Day, Every Night

Yolanda D. G. Andrews

ISBN 979-8-89243-629-8 (paperback)
ISBN 979-8-89428-321-0 (hardcover)
ISBN 979-8-89243-630-4 (digital)

Christian Faith Publishing
832 Park Avenue
Meadville, PA 16335
www.christianfaithpublishing.com

Printed in the United States of America

Dear Heavenly Father,

Thank You for Your instructions. As You awakened me from a deep sleep, I took notes as You gave me Your word. As You corrected me, I made changes.

I understand the power of prayer. Our job is to want the greatest for one another.

Grant me discipline. Help me establish boundaries. I want to be in line with Your will, Your way, and Your plan for my life. I harbor no regrets. I hold on to no anger. I trust You in all things.

"Give your entire attention to what God is doing right now, and don't get worked up about what may or may not happen tomorrow. God will help you deal with whatever hard things come up when the time comes" (Matthew 6:34 MSG).

Help us to get it, so we can live it, and give it.

I love You.

In Jesus' name,

Amen.

Dear Heavenly Father,

Thank You for my husband. It is because I made a vow to You that I choose to be a wife. I work every day to become better.

Thank You for our children. It is because of You, the ability to be fruitful and multiply, I am mom, mommie, mother, AND MAH. I work to become better every day.

It is because of the priceless gifts of creation, family, friends, neighbors, and enemies that I learn something every day.

I want to be a better me.

In Jesus' name I pray,

Amen.

Contents

May this tool help me, help all of us. Learn to take each day and focus on a specific area, and make it a matter of prayer. Eventually, you will be able to create your prayers for your "Every Day…Every Night."

Learn that true love comes from God. God first loved me. I love God, and I love myself. Now, I can love someone else. AGAPE.

Aim to bless God for His grace and mercy that protect the person on whom your prayers are focused. Ask God to free you from yourself. Don't punish yourself by waiting for the grave to grant you freedom.

Learn to be a friend. A friend is rare. A friend provides honesty and unconditional love—won't go along to get along. A friend wants to see you experience the best.

Give yourself better so you can be for the one you choose.

Clear your mind, open your heart, let's pray.

Chapter 1

Creation

Dear Heavenly Father,
I thank You for the creation of ___________.
Amen.

Our goal is to understand that God created each being for His purpose.

Every being did not come to birth through a perfect delivery. Sex is an act. God conceived you in love. Conception is a miracle. You are a complete, unique being made by Him, like Him.

Childhood shapes your future for adulthood. Your morals began to take shape based on your family's values, your emotions, inspirations, and understanding. As you get older, your values should strengthen toward greater, a better you.

Home should be a safe haven. For me, every member had a role and contributed to making my family. I was taught about and experienced God. The best storytelling I heard came from home. At the age of three, I was paying bills, banking, and grocery shopping. By the age of nine, I was writing checks. It doesn't take a genius to figure out what I chose as a career. At home, I learned, laughed, cried, and failed. Time will prove home's worth if you return to it for love, guidance, balance, sharing the details of your life, making more memories, and so much more.

If you survived "undesirable" living, turn it, make your environment better. I am sorry your home wasn't a glimpse of heaven. Experiences of hell should have come on the other side of your front door. We have to remember that our parents (guardians) did their best based on what they knew. If you feel they didn't instill in you the tools necessary to be better, be born again. Jesus taught us simply, "You're not listening. Let me say it again. Unless a person submits to this original creation—the 'wind-hovering-over-the-water' creation, the invisible moving the visible, a baptism into a new life—it's not possible to enter God's kingdom. When you look at a baby it's just that: a body you can look at and touch. But the person who takes shape within is formed by something you can't see and touch—the Spirit—and becomes a living spirit" (John 3:5–6 MSG).

Never use the excuse of negativity to be negative. Fight yourself to not repeat what you are used to seeing and living. How can you require a meeting to come to order, conduct it according to your strict agenda, but follow it up with an inappropriate comment to your colleague while standing at the microwave waiting for your meal to warm up?

If you don't know, ask. Learn. Exemplify.

Dear Heavenly Father,

Let the creation of ____________ be a blessing. Help ____________ choose a better way and be an example that is respected, starting internally and beyond.

Amen.

The Head

Chapter 2

Mind

Dear Heavenly Father,
Bless the thinking of _____________.
Amen.

So as a being thinketh, so they may do.

The world has created so much to distract us. It is amazing how the technology of today has changed from yesterday. When you take the good and turn it for the better, the technology of the world is essential. No longer do you have to think—well maybe it requires the proper thinking to phrase the search correctly.

Do yourself a favor: Before you use the tools of a computer, laptop, or cellular gadget to do the work, try God. Do you have a temptation, a weakness, a curiosity, or need encouragement? Acknowledge the issue in truth. Seek God. Accept His fix for it. Pray to deny your flesh daily. The little voice of temptation you hear within yourself is real. Beat your thoughts.

Studying the Bible teaches a learner, "So here's what I want you to do, God helping you: Take your everyday, ordinary life—your sleeping, eating, going-to-work, and walking-around life—and place it before God as an offering. Embracing what God does for you is the best thing you can do for Him. Don't become so well-adjusted to your culture that you fit into it without even thinking. Instead, fix your attention on God. You'll be changed from the inside out" (Romans 12:1–2 MSG).

CHANGE: six letters make a better you. Set boundaries to enhance your self-worth. Ask God for help. He starts within you.

No one lives a perfect life. Be careful of your thoughts. Just because you think about it doesn't mean you should do it. Don't allow your thinking to create a false truth, hindering you from receiving the truth. Don't allow your mind to wrestle with its thoughts, leading you into darkness in which you become lost, irrational, confused, and make the greatest mistake of your life. Be a better Christ-like being.

Dear Heavenly Father,
Let the thinking of _____________ be clear. Help _____________ to understand Your word and apply it to their life.
Amen.

Chapter 3

Ears

Dear Heavenly Father,
Bless the hearing of ______________.
Amen.

Do sounds make you wonder? Do you want to create things you have heard?

Be careful when you choose to imitate what you have heard.

Let your ears heed the voices of a wounded person. It is rare when you can seek the advice of a person who has gone through your experience, and they are able to hear the uniqueness of your experience. Find truth in knowing that most women can get pregnant, but no birth is the same. Find an accountable partner who is able to set aside self-issues and give you the best guidance as God instructs them to do so. This person doesn't choose sides. They choose God. To help a person be accountable to you, you have to tell the entire truth.

Sometimes, a person just needs to rant. They aren't looking for a response. I have learned, in times, to be a brick wall. I listen to the problem, don't give advice, but I pray on the matter for their good. Other times, I offer advice from God, not my flesh. I love you. I can't go to hell giving you advice from my flesh. The Bible warns us well: "Therefore consider carefully how you listen. Whoever has will be given more; whoever does not have, even what they think they have will be taken from them" (Luke 8:18 NIV).

Choose wisely the voices you allow to entertain your ears. Allow a television show to be just that. A good laugh is pleasing to the ears and delights the spirit. Don't allow this moment of pleasure to lead to a lifetime of misery.

Dear Heavenly Father,
Let the hearing of _____________ be attentive. Help _____________ to hear Your voice, Your will, Your way.
Amen.

Chapter 4

Eyes

Dear Heavenly Father,
Bless the seeing of ____________.
Amen.

The eyes are invaluable. Beauty is in the eyes, following the rules set by their owner. You can lock your eyes upon temptation and forget the world exists. Studies reveal humans perceive more than 75 percent of all their impressions (feelings) through the eyes. Learn to be greater than a surface scratcher. How great would it be if the eyes could truly give you a person's nature, virtues, and behavior? Don't allow your eyes to fool you.

The Bible teaches, "The eyes of your spirit allow revelation—light to enter into your being. If your heart is unclouded, the light floods in! But if your eyes are focused on money, the light cannot penetrate and darkness takes its place. How profound will be the darkness within you if the light of truth cannot enter" (Matthew 6:22–23 TPT).

If you can't stand on truth, you create your own darkness.

Live to find the beauty in God's creation. If He can give beauty to a tree that you don't nourish, what can our Father do for you? Find your self-beauty and never allow anyone, including you, to devalue it. Don't be guilty of thinking less of yourself, but think that is how others feel about you. Don't practice self-projecting. Remember, you can't force a person to see you as you want to be seen.

Control your eyes. Take pleasure in the beauty of your gifts. If you are blessed to have a family, pour into it and work to keep it healthy. The result is that every time you fix your eyes on it, you'll embrace the joy it brings and aim to protect it day-to-day.

Ask for your sight to be granted access to see the bigger picture.

Dear Heavenly Father,

Let the seeing of ___________ be greater than 20/15. Help ___________ to see Your good in all things.

Amen.

Chapter 5

Nose

Dear Heavenly Father,
Bless the smelling of ______________.
Amen.

Have you ever tried yoga? It is a great tool for controlling your breathing—inhale positivity, exhale negativity. It helps to focus your energy.

The nose is more than a breather. It helps the body identify, remember, and establish emotions. What it smells can enhance temptation. Why do you choose a particular fragrance? Because you want a smell that impresses and makes others wonder or ask, "What are you wearing?"

Your nose develops the quality of life you wish to experience. It shapes your mood; it can trigger thoughts—good and/or bad. Where you have to be careful is that you don't want your nose to tempt you and lead you away from God. I can remember that as a little girl, I thought if a man smelled good, he was the richest man and he lived the best life. As time passed, I learned a powerful smell doesn't eliminate struggles.

David asked, "God, come close. Come quickly! Open your ears—it's my voice you're hearing! Treat my prayer as sweet incense rising; my raised hands are my evening prayers" (Psalm 141:1–2 MSG).

The best aroma you can release into the air is the one God veri-fies. Giving off that smell to those who look up to you is contagious.

Dear Heavenly Father,
Let the smelling of ___________ have a godly effect. Help ___________'s smell be pleasant to You.
Amen.

Chapter 6

Tongue

Dear Heavenly Father,
Bless the tongue of ______________.
Amen.

The tongue is the most dangerous natural disaster you'll ever witness. As you live, I pray you learn that what you allow to part your lips sets up the environment for your life.

"This is scary: You can tame a tiger, but you can't tame a tongue—it's never been done. The tongue runs wild, a wanton killer. With our tongues we bless God our Father; with the same tongues we curse the very men and women he made in his image. Curses and blessings out of the same mouth" (James 3:7–10 MSG).

Are you a person who dominates the conversation? Have you ever thought "I shouldn't have said that"? Did you apologize? Do you think because you say it, it is what it must be? Do you possess the gift of tone (sound) control?

Leave babbling for brooks. It is not wise to tell everyone your story. Some that hear you sometimes prEy for you.

Be careful of how you choose to speak about another's life. What if you are heard by someone and you don't realize it? A damning word could have a lifelong effect if the hearer doesn't know how to turn your words into a stepping stone. Suicide can stem from little words that mature into deadly thoughts. 988 (Suicide and Crisis Hotline) and 1-800-799-7233 (the National Domestic Violence Hotline) are overwhelmed resources.

Choose better words.

Use your tongue to uplift and edify, correct, not poison. Do you know who the best audience is to deliver your secrets, stories, and/or problems? Set up a summit with God. Speak it out to Him first. He can tame your tongue better than you could ever dream. When it is time, you will be amazed at how God has changed your speech. Only then will you be ready to share your story to help others.

Dear Heavenly Father,

Let the tongue of _____________ be a blessing to many ears. Help the words from _____________'s tongue be acceptable to You.

Amen.

Tunnel to the Body

Chapter 7

Neck

Dear Heavenly Father,
Bless the neck of ______________.
Amen.

I think we have truly taken the neck for granted.

Did you know staring at your cellular device weakens the muscles of the neck and can cause tightness in the chest muscles?

The neck is the tunnel that leads from what occurs in the head (brain) to the rest of the body. It delivers nutrients, medications, poison, or whatever you give it. It is flexible; you can scan a location in a second.

Are you familiar with the practice of "talking out of both sides of the neck"? You know, using that flexibility to say one thing while executing another? You know, living one way in the light, living a different way in darkness?

I think one of the most difficult witnesses is when we are accountable to a friend and the advice isn't accepted. A person is allowed enough rope...continues to travel a road unpleasing to God...simply misusing themselves, ends up hanging self.

"My sins have been bound into a yoke, by his hands they were woven together. They have been hung on my neck, and the Lord has sapped my strength. He has given me into the hands of those I cannot withstand" (Lamentations 1:14 NIV).

Who is your greatest IN-UH?-ME (enemy)? Self. Self-doubt. Self-discouragement.

Understand that God is gracious. He doesn't force us to choose Him. Although He is jealous, He allows us to make a choice. Don't take your choices for granted and hang yourself.

Dear Heavenly Father,

Let the neck of ___________ be used to bring good to their body. Help ___________ choose to not be a double-talker, but a straight walker.

Amen.

Chapter 8

Heart

Dear Heavenly Father,
Bless the heart of ______________.
Amen.

The heart is the storehouse of compassion, emotional under-standing, and love. To know love is to feel the love of God and then love yourself. Once you master loving God, then yourself, you can love others.

How do you love yourself? You command your character to be upright when seen and unseen. Think wisely. Make healthy choices for your body. Set goals and achieve them. If you truly reflect on your last 365 days, if the only check mark you can make for yourself is living, you aren't living your purpose in God. Acknowledge your good and bad. How can you make good better? How can you bring peace to the bad?

If it helps, look in the mirror and tell yourself, "I love you," and hug yourself daily. It is important for the spirit to hear it and the body to feel it. If your significant other decides not to partake in the daily activity, no fret, you have given to you—self-love.

If you don't prioritize yourself, not limited to the examples stated above, you will never make a mate a priority.

Here's how the Bible lays it out: "Keep vigilant watch over your heart; that's where life starts. Don't talk out of both sides of your mouth; avoid careless banter, white lies, and gossip. Keep your eyes straight ahead; ignore all sideshow distractions. Watch your step, and the road will stretch out smooth before you. Look neither right nor left; leave evil in the dust" (Proverbs 4:23 MSG).

No one is eliminated from hurt—self-inflicted or from someone else. You can't measure hurt. Never seek revenge or think you can measure the punishment by the amount of pain you feel. Don't add greater pain to yourself. God knows. His judgment is just.

God is love. He said to guard your heart, not isolate it. Don't be so cold that you can't accept love. A hardened heart separates and divides. Jesus has to repeat Himself so they could truly understand.

"Jesus replied, 'You, too? Are you being willfully stupid? Don't you know that anything that is swallowed works its way through the intestines and is finally defecated? But what comes out of the mouth gets its start in the heart. It's from the heart that we vomit up evil arguments, murders, adulteries, fornications, thefts, lies, and cussing. That's what pollutes. Eating or not eating certain foods, washing or not washing our hands—that's neither here nor there'" (Matthew 15:16–20 MSG).

Get your heart and your mind in alignment. Find joy (for happiness is temporary) in the gifts God has allowed you to have: self-worth, marriage, family, and loved ones. Never use weapons of love destruction like silence (absence) and distance (space). Shutdowns are a practice of the government. Quitting leads to failure. Don't quit on you or yours. If God wants otherwise, He will whisper it to you.

Remember, life is like a drum with a set of drumsticks. You can invite someone to play their drumsticks with you and your drum. Never give your drumsticks away.

Use time wisely to receive God's love and give God's love.

Dear Heavenly Father,

Let the heart of ___________ be full of Your love. As You have shown compassion and empathy to us, let ___________ duplicate You.

Amen.

Chapter 9

Hands

Dear Heavenly Father,
Bless the hands of ______________.
Amen.

Be careful what you allow your hands to touch. One touch is all it takes. One stroke in the right place could lead to the wrong ending.

The Bible references how the hands were miraculously used to heal, cast out, or how one touch of His garment made a difference. Why do we choose to use our hands against His will? If you are blessed to have the use of both hands, use them to teach, worship, give an appropriate hug, a loving handshake, make a difference, and leave a powerful legacy.

I can recall an impression I made that didn't require a response. Hours after a meeting I had, a colleague said to me, "You have a great handshake."

I said, "I wanted you to feel 'I love you.' You never know what a person is going through. If you didn't feel 'I love you' today, may you feel it from my handshake."

He said, "I felt it. I love you too."

Make a request to God. Ask the Lord to lay His hand upon you. Ezra declared, "Because the hand of the Lord my God was on me, I took courage and…" (Ezra 7:28 NIV).

When you finally realize God's hand is on you, you realize He has filled you with His courage. What will you do NEXT?

Make sure your courageous NEXT touch is pleasing to God.

Dear Heavenly Father,

Let the hands of __________ be a powerful representation of You. May __________'s touch leave an everlasting, godly impression.

Amen.

Chapter 10

Abdomen

Dear Heavenly Father,
Bless the abdomen of ______________.
Amen.

What a powerful section of the body! I have to be honest; I rarely use the term *abdomen*. I usually say *the stomach area*. This area of the body houses the stomach, the intestines, the colon, the liver, the pancreas, the ovaries, and so much more. It stores nourishment, gluttony, life, discernment, transformation, and pain. Why are so many deadly diagnoses, illnesses, inflammations, and pains linked to this area of the body? Are we housing unresolved issues here, allowing them to fester, resulting in our deterioration?

I once attended a spiritual retreat and was totally in until we got to the part when the instructor touched my stomach and said, "Let it go, sister." I looked at him like he was crazy. I wasn't holding on to anything. I was fine. I witnessed the release of "the blaaah" from mouths, and it scared me. I didn't realize people with a discerning spirit could sense your burdens without you saying a word. I didn't realize your hurts and pains take up residency within your body. That instructor saw something in me. Either I didn't realize something was there or I was ignoring my truth?

Life happens. Choices bring consequences. The sooner you are able to accept it, deal with it, and then heal from it, the better quality of life you will have. Never store up so much toxicity that you crash and burn. The Bible teaches us well: "You can't whitewash your sins and get by with it; you find mercy by admitting and leaving them" (Proverbs 28:13 MSG).

Stop allowing everything to linger, causing harm to you. Forgiveness is a gift to self. Being right? Being wrong? Try being God-like. Use differences to learn and become better. Bring His peace to every situation, and God will reward you for it.

Dear Heavenly Father,

Let the abdomen of ______________ be a place of healthy storage for the organs it contains. Let each part perform its duty without adding any heaviness to accumulate from unresolved pain.

Amen.

Below the Belt

Chapter 11

Accessory

Dear Heavenly Father,
Bless the accessory of ______________.
Amen.

Sexual appetite, addictions, and falsehoods: have you established your desires about sex from what your eyes have seen and your ears have heard? I must be honest: movies and videos create the best screens. I wonder how many takes they scratched to give us the most appealing view.

God created the experience of sexual intimacy as a precious, private, and sacred gift. It grants pleasure. It produces life. It's a reward. It is the greatest form of two becoming one, figuring out what is best for them. Unfortunately, flesh has caused us to manipulate it. We take it when both parties don't agree. We can't commit to enjoying it with one partner. If you hold respect for one another, don't kiss and tell. If you can't commit, respect God, respect yourself, and do it the right way. That's character.

Your spirit feels it when your relationship is true; you won't hold back from giving yourself completely to your one. The Bible recorded it clearly, "Honor marriage, and guard the sacredness of sexual intimacy between wife and husband. God draws a firm line against casual and illicit sex" (Hebrews 13:1–44 MSG). I don't judge your choices. That is the job of God.

Do you battle with self-control (emotions and desires)? Try fasting. Studies prove that abstaining from an activity for more than twenty days becomes a habit. People think fasting is only giving up food. I used to say, if God wanted us to not eat, He wouldn't have created food. Fasting is giving up something that you know is not good for you. Giving it up will be hard but worth it. To control self, is to control your flesh. What do you need to release? Are you ready to release it? Start now.

Remember, love doesn't grow from your accessory. The accessory enhances the relationship. Be careful where you place your priorities. There is no replacement for your accessory.

I wish the greatest sexual experience God created for all beings at the right time, in the right place, and with the right person.

Dear Heavenly Father,
Let the accessory of _____________ be satisfied according to Your design.
Amen.

Chapter 12

Knees

Dear Heavenly Father,
Bless the knees of ______________.
Amen.

The knees are the most stressed joints of the body. They help the legs get you to where you need to go under the instruction of God. You know, where God leads me, I will follow.

The Bible teaches that the knee is a symbol of strength. Do you have strong knees? Which do you prefer to do: bend your knees to enjoy a dance move or fall upon them to pray for your enemies? How about both?

Be careful of the environment in which you allow your spirit to sit and engage. Take it as a matter of pride that you are allowed to choose your audience. It is not degrading when you select: "I choose not to sit there because I don't like the conversations they discuss when we eat lunch." However, if you choose to sit and eat, can you be the voice to help bring the conversation to a tolerable level for all? There is no conversation too difficult or a situation too critical if God says you should be there. Make a difference.

We are in this world because God has our time date-stamped. We are not here by luck. The Bible records, "I know what I'm doing. I have it all planned out—plans to take care of you, not abandon you, plans to give you the future you hope for" (Jeremiah 29:11 MSG).

The question you must ask yourself: Are your knees assisting you in getting where you need to be according to the plan God has for your life?

Dear Heavenly Father,
Let the knees of _____________ be used to support the body, aiming to fulfill its purpose. May one of the most powerful encounters _____________ has with You be on bended knees.
Amen.

Chapter 13

Feet

Dear Heavenly Father,
Bless the feet of ___________.
Amen.

Be careful of the places you allow your feet to take you.

Do you consider your feet the dirtiest part of your body? Do you treat them as such?

Teachers often communicate to us that the footsteps of a being are ordered.

"The Lord makes firm the steps of the one who delights in Him; though he may stumble, He will not fall, for the Lord upholds him with His hand" (Psalm 37:23–24 NIV).

Through your heart, the Father instructs you. The heart instructs the mind. The mind instructs the feet. If you can't follow the order, you can't live on purpose. Because God is gracious, He knows we will make mistakes. If we handle the mistakes correctly—repent, make amends, don't repeat—you know your feet stumble, He still allows you to use your feet and stand. Now that's grace.

We all don't reach the finish line at the same time. We don't reach maturity at the same time. Understanding God's Word takes time and a devotion to studying. For years, I would try to pick up the Bible and complain that it was too difficult to understand. I would try to read Revelations and get a headache. What a difference a translation makes! So what if you don't understand one translation? Try a different one. Remember, the root of God's Word doesn't change. A translation is a matter of interpretation. It took years for me to understand that.

Making a vow to God to follow His plan for your life illustrates His mercy and grace in your walk. Give up the notion of "my way." Display His way.

Are you blessed to use your feet to walk in Him? Try a walk in nature. See what the clouds reveal to you. Hear what the birds chirp to you. Smell the fragrance the flowers blessingly release to you.

Dear Heavenly Father,

Let the feet of ___________ be used for the enlightenment of You. May ___________ stand in truth. May ___________ walk in Your glory.

Amen.

Until Next...

I just want to help us know it, feel it, and share it.

You are loved by God. He requires us to love.

The ultimate goal is God's "Well done..." I believe our choices grant us the ability to experience heaven on earth. Sometimes we make choices that lead us closer to Him; other times, we stray away. Choose wisely.

Pray not to go too far out, that you can't return to Him.

Have you been called out of your name, reduced in your title, felt hate instead of love, not one kind word or gesture aimed at you? Your response: Just love and let God do what He does.

Sometimes we ask ourselves, Why me? Why not me? If it weren't for the experiences of life, we wouldn't have an opportunity to show ourselves approved.

Since God has blessed your creation, may He bless your mind (thinking), ears (hearing), eyes (seeing), nose (smelling), tongue (talking), neck (tunnel), heart (loving), hands (touching), abdomen (storing), accessory (desiring), knees (supporting), and feet (walking).

Do you get it? I love you from your head to your feet. I don't love you too (also). My love doesn't depend on you loving me back. I want to love like God loves.

Do you get it? God hates some actions. God loves the actor. I choose to act like Him.

Moving forward: "And now here's what I want you to do: Tell the truth, the whole truth, when you speak. Do the right thing by one another, both personally and in your courts. Don't cook up plans to take unfair advantage of others. Don't do or say what isn't so. I hate all that stuff. Keep your lives simple and honest. Decree of God" (Zechariah 8:16–17 MSG).

Make everything a matter of prayer. Put God in the center of everything.

Start with God, then yourself, and move forward.

Be blessed.

I love you.